# SUZUKI®
# HARP ENSEMBLE MUSIC

Volume 1

SECOND HARP ACCOMPANIMENTS

*By Barbara Meixner*

*Edited by Mary Kay Waddington*

# CONTENTS






ISBN 0-87487-753-9
1 3 5 7 8 6 4 2

*Cover Design: Aean Pinheiro*

**Summy-Birchard Inc.**
exclusively distributed by
Warner Bros. Publications Inc.
15800 N.W. 48th Avenue
Miami, Florida 33014

# "Twinkle, Twinkle, Little Star" Variations

## Variation A

Shinichi Suzuki

# "Twinkle, Twinkle, Little Star" Variations

## Variation B

Shinichi Suzuki

# "Twinkle, Twinkle, Little Star" Variations

## Variation C

Shinichi Suzuki

# Lavender's Blue

Folk Song

# Lightly Row

## Octaves

Folk Song

# The Honeybee

Folk Song

# Mary Had A Little Lamb

Folk Song

# Crickets' Song

M.K. Waddington

# Lightly Row

## Alberti Bass

Folk Song

# London Bridge

Folk Song

# Go Tell Aunt Rhody

Folk Song

# Silent Night

F. Gruber

# Long, Long Ago

T.H. Bayly

# Little Playmates

F.X. Chwatal

# Chant Arabe

## Pedal Harp

Anonymous

# Good-bye to Winter

Folk Song

# The Good Little King of Yvetot

Folk Song

# Andante

## Accompaniment 1

M.K. Waddington

11
p
14
rit. e cresc.
17
mp
a tempo
rit.

# Andante
## Accompaniment 2

M.K. Waddington

# Christmas-Day Secrets

T. Dutton

10
p
15
mp
F♮
20
p
rit.

# Allegro

In this music, a dot over a note indicates a crisp,
light attack rather than shortened duration.

Shinichi Suzuki

# Musette
## Pedal Harp

Anonymous

# Gigue

M.K. Waddington

13
4 3 2 1
17
21
4 3 2 1